AIR FRYER COOBOOK FOR BEGINNERS

Healthy Meals Fast Using Your Instant Pot Air Fryer - Complete Solution to Air Fry, Roast, Bakes, Broil and much more!!

BY

MAYA DAVIS

of the use of information contained within this document, including, but not limited to, - errors, omissions, or inaccuracies.

INTRODUCTION

When it comes to an electric cooking appliance, the very first step is to prepare the device for cooking. It needs to be cleaned inside out with a clean piece of cloth then plugging in to examine if all the parts are working perfectly. Here is how you can cook well using your Instant Vortex Air Fryer Oven:

1. First, plug in the device and switch it ON. The led display will be lit up, indicating that the device is working.

2. Since this vortex oven quickly preheats, you need to prepare the food first and keep it ready for cooking before preheating.

3. Place the Drip pan inside, at the bottom of the oven to protect its base from food particles and grease.

4. Use the Air fryer basket, baking pan, roasting pan, rotisserie rod, or any other suitable accessory to place the food inside according to the instructions of a particular recipe.

5. You can insert up to three trays into the oven to accommodate your food in three layers if needed.

6. When the food is ready, you can preheat

the appliance. Close its lid and press the desired cooking operation: Bake, Roast, Broil, Air Fry, Dehydrate or Reheat.

7. By selecting this program, the device will show the preset temperature and cooking time on the display; you can change it by using the "+" or "- "keys for temperature and time to increase or decrease the values, respectively.

8. Press the start button to initiate preheating. The display timer does not start ticking until the appliance is preheated. When it reaches the desired temperature, the display will blink "FOOD" and beep to show if the device is preheated.

9. Situate the food inside and close the lid to initiate cooking.

10.   When the display says FLIP, turn

or toss the food place inside the oven.

11.   Once the cooking function is completed, the device will beep to indicate that the food is now ready to serve.

12.   After each session of cooking, remove all the trays and accessories from inside the oven and wash them either in the dishwasher or with some soap water. Dry them well, then use them whenever needed.

13.   Make sure to wash, clean, and reinsert the dripping pan every time.

Tips & Tricks for Your Air Fryer Oven

The Instant Plus Vortex Air Fry Oven is specially designed to give all its users easy cleaning and smart maintenance.

1. Use a dry cloth to rub off the exterior of

the oven.

2. Once the cooking session is completed, unplug the oven and leave it on your countertop to cool down.

3. The interior of the oven can be cleaned with a lightly damp cloth. Simply rub off the walls and remove all the grease and food particles, if any.

4. Once it is cooled completely, remove its removable door and clean it well using a wet cloth. Don't scrub it hard.

5. Take out all the removable items from inside and wash them thoroughly using soap water. It is best to wash and dry them in your dishwasher.

6. Fix the oven door back into its place along with all the accessories, and the device is ready to use again.

An air fryer is a countertop appliance used for cooking almost everything from fries to meat to vegetables. You will find the settings, heating element, and fan at the top, as well as a basket at the bottom that appears as a drawer. The air fryer blows heat around the space, which compresses the outer surface of the food.

Air fryers can give food a crisp and crisp texture with only a fraction of the oil needed for frying. This is possible because fryers transfer heat to food via liquid fats. But air fryers transfer heat by convection, where a fan quickly circulates hot air and sprays tiny droplets of oil around the food.

The air fryer heats food in all directions by blowing hot air around the container. As long as your food is not stacked in, they cook evenly on all sides.

The air moves much faster in a fryer than in the oven, and in a confined space, which affects the duration and regularity of cooking.

The technique of air circulation is called convection. This is the same process that a convection oven uses to make food cook faster and more evenly. Combining this with little oil, an air fryer can give the food a texture cooked inside and crisp on the outside, like a deep fryer.

"The circulation of warm air and the 360-degree exposure to food mimics the result of frying by creating a crisp and golden layer."

The convection mechanism means that air fryers only need one tablespoon of oil to give the food a deep-fried texture. And since you do not use a lot of oil at the beginning, the result is that air-fried foods absorb much less fat than their deep-fried counterparts. "Even frying requires several tablespoons for 1/2 cup of oil. And more fat equals more calories in general.

GENERAL TSO'S CAULIFLOWER

Total Time

Prep: 25 min. Cook: 20 min.

Makes

4 servings

Ingredients:

- Oil for profound fat fricasseeing

- 1/2 cup generally useful flour
- 1/2 cup cornstarch
- 1 teaspoon salt
- 1 teaspoon preparing powder
- 3/4 cup club pop
- 1 medium head cauliflower, cut into 1-inch florets (around 6 cups)

SAUCE:

- 1/4 cup squeezed orange
- 3 tablespoons sugar
- 3 tablespoons soy sauce
- 3 tablespoons vegetable stock
- 2 tablespoons rice vinegar
- 2 teaspoons sesame oil
- 2 teaspoons cornstarch
- 2 tablespoons canola oil

- 2 to 6 dried pasilla or other hot chilies, cleaved
- 3 green onions, white part minced, green part daintily cut
- 3 garlic cloves, minced
- 1 teaspoon ground new gingerroot
- 1/2 teaspoon ground orange get-up-and-go
- 4 cups hot cooked rice

Directions:

1. In an electric skillet or profound fryer, heat oil to 375°. Consolidate flour, cornstarch, salt, and heating powder. Mix in club soft drink just until mixed (hitter will be slender). Plunge florets, a couple at once, into

the player and fry until cauliflower is delicate and covering is light dark colored, 8-10 minutes. Channel on paper towels.

2. For the sauce, whisk together the initial six fixings; race in cornstarch until smooth.

3. In a huge pot, heat canola oil over medium-high warmth. Include chilies; cook and mix until fragrant, 2 minutes. Include a white piece of onions, garlic, ginger, and orange get-up-and-go; cook until fragrant, around 1 moment. Mix soy sauce blend; add to the pan. Heat to the point of boiling; cook and mix until thickened, 4 minutes.

4. Add cauliflower to sauce; hurl to cover. Present with rice; sprinkle with daintily cut green onions.

ROASTED CURRIED CHICKPEAS AND CAULIFLOWER

Total Time

Prep: 15 min. Bake: 30 min.

Makes

4 servings

Ingredients:

- 2 pounds potatoes (around 4 medium), stripped and cut into 1/2-inch solid shapes
- 1 little head cauliflower, broken into florets (around 3 cups)
- 1 can (15 ounces) chickpeas or garbanzo beans, flushed and depleted
- 3 tablespoons olive oil
- 2 teaspoons curry powder
- 3/4 teaspoon salt
- 1/4 teaspoon pepper
- 3 tablespoons minced crisp cilantro or parsley

Directions:

1. Preheat broiler to 400°. Spot initial 7 fixings in an enormous bowl; hurl to cover. Move to a 15x10x1-in. preparing containers covered with cooking shower.

2. Cook until vegetables are delicate, 30-35 minutes, blending every so often. Sprinkle with cilantro.

CHICKPEA MINT TABBOULEH

Total Time

Prep/Total Time: 30 min.

Makes

4 servings

Ingredients:

- 1 cup bulgur
- 2 cups of water
- 1 cup new or solidified peas (around 5 ounces), defrosted
- 1 can (15 ounces) chickpeas or garbanzo beans, washed and depleted
- 1/2 cup minced new parsley
- 1/4 cup minced new mint
- 1/4 cup olive oil

- 2 tablespoons julienned delicate sun-dried tomatoes (not stuffed in oil)
- 2 tablespoons lemon juice
- 1/2 teaspoon salt
- 1/4 teaspoon pepper

Directions:

1. In a huge pot, consolidate bulgur and water; heat to the point of boiling. Decrease heat; stew, secured, 10 minutes. Mix in crisp or solidified peas; cook, secured, until bulgur and peas are delicate, around 5 minutes.

2. Move to an enormous bowl. Mix in outstanding fixings. Serve warm, or refrigerate and serve cold.

CREAMY CAULIFLOWER PAKORA SOUP

Total Time

Prep: 20 min. Cook: 20 min.

Makes

8 servings (3 quarts)

Ingredients:

- 1 huge head cauliflower, cut into little florets
- 5 medium potatoes, stripped and diced
- 1 huge onion, diced
- 4 medium carrots, stripped and diced
- 2 celery ribs, diced
- 1 container (32 ounces) vegetable stock
- 1 teaspoon garam masala
- 1 teaspoon garlic powder
- 1 teaspoon ground coriander
- 1 teaspoon ground turmeric
- 1 teaspoon ground cumin
- 1 teaspoon pepper
- 1 teaspoon salt

- 1/2 teaspoon squashed red pepper chips
- Water or extra vegetable stock
- New cilantro leaves
- Lime wedges, discretionary

Directions:

1. In a Dutch stove over medium-high warmth, heat initial 14 fixings to the point of boiling. Cook and mix until vegetables are delicate, around 20 minutes. Expel from heat; cool marginally. Procedure in groups in a blender or nourishment processor until smooth. Modify consistency as wanted with water (or extra stock). Sprinkle with new cilantro. Serve

hot, with lime wedges whenever wanted.

2. Stop alternative: Before including cilantro, solidify cooled soup in cooler compartments. To utilize, in part defrost in cooler medium-term. Warmth through in a pan, blending every so often and including a little water if fundamental. Sprinkle with cilantro. Whenever wanted, present with lime wedges.

SMOKY CAULIFLOWER

Total Time

Prep/Total Time: 30 min.

Makes

8 servings

Ingredients:

- 1 huge head cauliflower, broken into 1-inch florets (around 9 cups)

- 2 tablespoons olive oil
- 1 teaspoon smoked paprika
- 3/4 teaspoon salt
- 2 garlic cloves, minced
- 2 tablespoons minced new parsley

Directions:

1. Spot cauliflower in an enormous bowl. Consolidate the oil, paprika, and salt. Shower over cauliflower; hurl to cover. Move to a 15x10x1-in. Preparing container. Prepare, revealed, at 450° for 10 minutes.

2. Mix in garlic. Prepare 14 minutes longer or until cauliflower is delicate and daintily cooked, mixing

every so often. Sprinkle with
parsley.

SPICE TRADE BEANS AND BULGUR

Total Time

Prep: 30 min. Cook: 3-1/2 hours

Makes

10 servings

Ingredients:

- 3 tablespoons canola oil, isolated
- 2 medium onions, slashed
- 1 medium sweet red pepper, slashed
- 5 garlic cloves, minced
- 1 tablespoon ground cumin
- 1 tablespoon paprika
- 2 teaspoons ground ginger
- 1 teaspoon pepper

- 1/2 teaspoon ground cinnamon
- 1/2 teaspoon cayenne pepper
- 1-1/2 cups bulgur
- 1 can (28 ounces) squashed tomatoes
- 1 can (14-1/2 ounces) diced tomatoes, undrained
- 1 container (32 ounces) vegetable juices
- 2 tablespoons darker sugar
- 2 tablespoons soy sauce
- 1 can (15 ounces) garbanzo beans or chickpeas, flushed and depleted
- 1/2 cup brilliant raisins
- Minced crisp cilantro, discretionary

Directions:

1. In a large skillet, heat 2 tablespoons oil over medium-high warmth. Include onions and pepper; cook and mix until delicate, 3-4 minutes. Include garlic and seasonings; cook brief longer. Move to a 5-qt. slow cooker.

2. In the same skillet, heat remaining oil over medium-high warmth. Include bulgur; cook and mix until daintily caramelized, 2-3 minutes or until softly sautéed.

3. Include bulgur, tomatoes, stock, darker sugar, and soy sauce to slow cooker. Cook, secured, on low 3-4 hours or until bulgur is delicate. Mix in beans and raisins; cook 30

minutes longer. Whenever wanted, sprinkle with cilantro.

TOFU CHOW MEIN

Total Time

Prep: 15 min. + standing Cook: 15 min.

Makes

4 servings

Ingredients:

- 8 ounces uncooked entire wheat holy messenger hair pasta
- 3 tablespoons sesame oil, separated
- 1 bundle (16 ounces) extra-firm tofu
- 2 cups cut new mushrooms
- 1 medium sweet red pepper, julienned
- 1/4 cup decreased sodium soy sauce
- 3 green onions daintily cut

Directions:

1. Cook pasta as per bundle headings. Channel; flush with cold water and channel once more. Hurl with 1 tablespoon oil; spread onto a preparing sheet and let remain around 60 minutes.

2. In the meantime, cut tofu into 1/2-in. 3D shapes and smudge dry. Enclose by a clean kitchen towel; place on a plate and refrigerate until prepared to cook.

3. In an enormous skillet, heat 1 tablespoon oil over medium warmth. Include pasta, spreading equitably; cook until the base is

daintily caramelized, around 5 minutes. Expel from skillet.

4. In the same skillet, heat remaining oil over medium-high warmth; pan sear mushrooms, pepper, and tofu until mushrooms are delicate, 3-4 minutes. Include pasta and soy sauce; hurl and heat through. Sprinkle with green onions.

CHARD AND WHITE BEAN PASTA

Total Time

Prep: 20 min. Cook: 20 min.

Makes

8 servings

Ingredients:

- 1 bundle (12 ounces) uncooked entire wheat or darker rice penne pasta
- 2 tablespoons olive oil

- 4 cups cut leeks (a white bit as it were)
- 1 cup cut sweet onion
- 4 garlic cloves, cut
- 1 tablespoon minced crisp savvy or 1 teaspoon scoured sage
- 1 enormous sweet potato, stripped and cut into 1/2-inch solid shapes
- 1 medium bundle Swiss chard (around 1 pound), cut into 1-inch cuts
- 1 can (15-1/2 ounces) extraordinary northern beans, flushed and depleted
- 3/4 teaspoon salt
- 1/4 teaspoon bean stew powder

- 1/4 teaspoon squashed red pepper drops
- 1/8 teaspoon ground nutmeg
- 1/8 teaspoon pepper
- 1/3 cup finely slashed crisp basil
- 1 tablespoon balsamic vinegar
- 2 cups marinara sauce, warmed

Directions:

1. Cook pasta as indicated by bundle headings. Channel, holding 3/4 cup pasta water.

2. In a 6-qt. stockpot, heat oil over medium warmth; saute leeks and onion until delicate, 5-7 minutes. Include garlic and sage; cook and mix 2 minutes.

3. Include potato and chard; cook, secured, over medium-low warmth 5 minutes. Mix in beans, seasonings and held pasta water; cook, secured, until potato and chard are delicate, around 5 minutes.

4. Include pasta, basil, and vinegar; hurl and warmth through. Present with sauce.

KRA ROASTED WITH SMOKED PAPRIKA

Total Time

Prep: 5 min. Cook: 30 min.

Makes

12 servings

Ingredients:

- 3 pounds new okra cases
- 3 tablespoons olive oil
- 3 tablespoons lemon juice
- 1-1/2 teaspoons smoked paprika
- 1/4 teaspoon garlic powder
- 3/4 teaspoon salt
- 1/2 teaspoon pepper

Directions:

1. Preheat stove to 400°. Hurl together all fixings. Mastermind in a 15x10x1-in. Heating skillet; cook until okra is delicate and softly sautéed, 30-35 minutes.

GARDEN VEGETABLE AND HERB SOUP

Total Time

Prep: 20 min. Cook: 30 min.

Makes

8 servings (2 quarts)

Ingredients:

- 2 tablespoons olive oil
- 2 medium onions, hacked
- 2 huge carrots, cut
- 1 pound red potatoes (around 3 medium), cubed
- 2 cups of water
- 1 can (14-1/2 ounces) diced tomatoes in sauce
- 1-1/2 cups vegetable soup

- 1-1/2 teaspoons garlic powder
- 1 teaspoon dried basil
- 1/2 teaspoon salt
- 1/2 teaspoon paprika
- 1/4 teaspoon dill weed
- 1/4 teaspoon pepper
- 1 medium yellow summer squash, split and cut

  1 medium zucchini, split and cut

Directions:

1. In a huge pan, heat oil over medium warmth. Include onions and carrots; cook and mix until onions are delicate, 4-6 minutes. Include potatoes and cook 2 minutes. Mix in water, tomatoes, juices, and seasonings. Heat to the point of boiling. Diminish heat; stew, revealed, until potatoes and carrots are delicate, 9 minutes.

2. Include yellow squash and zucchini; cook until vegetables are delicate, 9 minutes longer. Serve or, whenever wanted, puree blend in clusters,

including extra stock until desired consistency is accomplished.

CAULIFLOWER WITH ROASTED ALMOND AND PEPPER DIP

Ingredients:
Total Time
Prep: 40 min. Bake: 35 min.
Makes
10 servings (2-1/4 cups dip)
Ingredients:

- 10 cups water
- 1 cup olive oil, isolated
- 3/4 cup sherry or red wine vinegar, isolated
- 3 tablespoons salt
- 1 cove leaf
- 1 tablespoon squashed red pepper drops

- 1 enormous head cauliflower
- 1/2 cup entire almonds, toasted
- 1/2 cup delicate entire wheat or white bread morsels, toasted
- 1/2 cup fire-simmered squashed tomatoes
- 1 container (8 ounces) broiled sweet red peppers, depleted
- 2 tablespoons minced new parsley
- 2 garlic cloves
- 1 teaspoon sweet paprika
- 1/2 teaspoon salt
- 1/4 teaspoon newly ground pepper

Directions:

1. In a 6-qt. stockpot, bring water, 1/2 cup oil, 1/2 cup sherry, salt, sound

leaf and pepper pieces to a bubble. Include cauliflower. Diminish heat; stew, revealed, until a blade effectively embeds into focus, 15-20 minutes, turning part of the way through cooking. Evacuate with an opened spoon; channel well on paper towels.

2. Preheat broiler to 450°. Spot cauliflower on a lubed wire rack in a 15x10x1-in. heating dish. Prepare on a lower broiler rack until dim brilliant, 39 minutes.

3. In the meantime, place almonds, bread morsels, tomatoes, cooked peppers, parsley, garlic, paprika, salt, and pepper in a nourishment

processor; beat until finely cleaved. Include remaining sherry; process until mixed. Keep preparing while step by step, including remaining oil in a constant flow. Present with cauliflower.

SPICY GRILLED BROCCOLI

Total Time

Prep: 20 min. + standing Grill: 10 min.

Makes

6 servings

Ingredients:

- 2 packs broccoli
- MARINADE:
- 1/2 cup olive oil
- 1/4 cup juice vinegar
- 1 teaspoon onion powder
- 1 teaspoon garlic powder
- 1 teaspoon smoked paprika
- 1/2 teaspoon salt

- 1/2 teaspoon squashed red pepper pieces
- 1/4 teaspoon pepper

Direction:

1. Cut every broccoli pack into 6 pieces. In a 6-qt. stockpot, place a steamer container more than 1 in. of water. Spot broccoli in a bushel. Heat water to the point of boiling. Decrease warmth to keep up a stew; steam, secured, 4-6 minutes or until fresh delicate.

2. In an enormous bowl, whisk marinade fixings until mixed. Include broccoli; delicately hurl to

cover. Let stand, secured, 15 minutes.

3. Channel broccoli, saving marinade. Flame broil broccoli, secured, over medium warmth, or cook 4 in from heat 6-8 minutes or until broccoli is delicate, turning once. Whenever wanted, present withheld marinade.

SAUTEED SQUASH WITH TOMATOES AND ONIONS

Total Time

Prep/Total Time: 20 min.

Makes

8 servings

Ingredients:

- 2 tablespoons olive oil
- 1 medium onion, finely hacked
- 4 medium zucchini, hacked
- 2 huge tomatoes, finely hacked
- 1 teaspoon salt
- 1/4 teaspoon pepper

Directions:

1. In a huge skillet, heat oil over medium-high warmth. Include onion; cook and mix until delicate, 2-4 minutes. Include zucchini; cook and mix 3 minutes.
2. Mix in tomatoes, salt, and pepper; cook and mix until squash is delicate, 4-6 minutes longer. Present with an opened spoon.

HEALING MUSHROOM SOUP NEW INSTANT POT

Total Time

Prep: 20 min. Cook: 1 half-hour.

Makes

10 servings (2 quarts)

Ingredients:

- 1 box cut white mushrooms (226 grams)
- 1/2 box Shtik mushrooms (226 grams), stems expelled, end disposed of and stems hacked
- 100 grams Enoki mushrooms (Half of a little pack)
- One medium white onion, cleaved
- 3 celery stalks, cleaved
- 3 garlic cloves, crushed
- 1 carrot, cut into slight circles or slashed into shapes
- Little bunch watercress, cleaved
- Bone stock to arrive at the 6 cup mark within the Instapot

- 3 tbsp grease or warmth stable fat of decision
- 1 tbsp minced crisp ginger
- 1 tbsp fish sauce
- 2 crisp straight leafs
- 1 tsp dried oregano
- 1/2 tsp dried thyme
- 1 tsp nectar
- 1-2 tbsp collagen* (discretionary)
- Juice from half of a lime
- Foul salt to taste
- Collagen Hydrolysate (Green holder if utilizing Great Lakes brand)

Directions:

1. Attachment in the Instant Pot and press the "Sauté" work.

2. Include your fat of decision, onions, carrots, and celery to the pot and sauté until they start to relax and turn translucent. Include a liberal spot of foul salt to bring out flavors and discharge juices.

3. Following five minutes, include the white mushrooms and keep on cooking until delicate, 5 additional minutes.

4. When the veggies are delicate, include the garlic and ginger, mix and cook for a moment or two until fragrant.

5. Include the fish sauce, sound leaves, and flavors and consolidate well.

6. Add the rest of the mushrooms to the pot, Shiitake, and Enoki
7. Pour in the stock to the 6 cup stamp and tenderly mix to consolidate.
8. Press the "Keep Warm/Cancel" catch to stop the sauté mode.
9. Spot the top on the Instant Pot and lock the cover. Contort the steam discharge handle on the cover to "Fixing".

More Directions:

1. Press the "manual" catch to switch the cooking mode. Set the cooking time for 7 minutes. Note that the soup will cook for longer than seven minutes as it requires some

investment for the compel cooker to arrive at the wanted weight. The brief clock will begin once a legitimate weight is accomplished. When the soup is finished cooking, the Instant Pot will consequently change to the "Keep Warm" mode and will flag finished with signals. When you hear the blares, the soup has cooked for the full seven minutes at the total weight. Give the soup a chance to stay in the "Keep Warm" mode for 10 minutes and afterward press "Drop."

2. Turn the steam discharge handle on the cover to "Venting." I generally put on my broiler glove as a

precautionary measure as a modest quantity of steam will escape from the venting opening. When the weight has discharged, cautiously open the Instant Pot.

3. Mix in the nectar and the juice of half of new lime. Taste for flavoring. Include progressively foul salt (if necessary) Include collagen powder, if utilizing, to include additional protein.

4. Tenderly mix in the cleaved watercress and let sit for one moment.

5. Scoop soup into bowls. On the off chance that you are attempting to build you solid fats, mix in one tbsp

to each bowl of either grass
encouraged to spread, coconut oil,
fed fat or ghee before serving.

PEACHES AND CREAM OATMEAL INSTANT POT

Total Time

Prep: 15 min. Cook: 60 min.

Makes

12 servings (8 quarts)

Ingredients:

- 2 ready peaches, set + hacked

- 1/4 cup unadulterated maple syrup
- 1/4 tsp ground cinnamon
- 1/8 cup separated water
- 2 cups nut milk of decision
- 1 cup separated water
- Touch of ocean salt
- Cinnamon stick (discretionary)
- 1 cup natural without gluten steel-cut oats
- 1-4 tbsp grass-encouraged spread (or coconut oil for dairy-free)
- 1/4-1/2 cup full fat cream (or coconut milk for dairy-free)
- Extra cream or dairy-free milk of decision for serving
- Extra unadulterated maple syrup for serving

- 1-3 new ready peaches, set and diced
- Hacked nuts, seeds or dried product of choice for fixings

Directions:

1. In a blender, puree the hacked peaches, maple syrup, cinnamon, and 1/8 cup water. Empty peach puree into an estimating cup.

2. Fitting in the Instant Pot. Include the oats, 2 cups nut milk, 1 cup sifted the water, a touch of ocean salt and a discretionary cinnamon stick.

3. Mix and afterward place the top on the Instant Pot and lock the cover.

Bend the steam discharge handle on the cover to "Fixing".

4. Press the "manual" catch to pick the cooking mode. Utilize the bolts to change the cooking time to 3 minutes. Note that the cereal will cook for longer than 3 minutes as it requires some investment for the constrain cooker to arrive at the wanted weight. The brief clock will begin once an appropriate weight is accomplished.

5. When the cereal is finished cooking, the Instant Pot will naturally change to the "Keep Warm" mode and will flag finished with signals. When you hear the blares, the oats

have cooked for the full 3 minutes at total weight. Give the oats a chance to stay in the "Keep Warm" mode until the weight normally discharges and afterward press "Drop."

6. Wind the steam discharge handle on the top to "Venting," but since you discharged the weight usually there will be no steam.

7. Open the Instant Pot and mix in necessary measure of margarine or coconut oil and the peach fluid from the blender. Taste and modify sweetness as per taste.

8. Let sit for a couple of moments to cool marginally at that point

include the 1/4-1/2 cup of cream or coconut/nut milk of decision

9. Overlay in crisp diced peaches and present with extra milk of choice and fixings of decision

ROASTED RED PEPPER AND CAULIFLOWER SOUP INSTANT POT

Total Time

Prep: 10 min. Cook: 56 min.

Makes

9 servings (5 quarts)

Ingredients:

- 1 head cauliflower, cut into florets
- 5 garlic cloves, crushed
- 4 green onions, slashed
- 1 340 ml container of simmered red peppers, diced (approx. 3 peppers)
- 1 14oz container of finely slashed tomatoes (I utilized Solo Pomodoro Mutti tomatoes)

- 2 huge carrots, diced
- 2 red shepherd peppers, seeded + diced
- 1/4 cup greens of decision (I utilized swiss chard), cut up into little strings or diced
- 1 tbsp smoked paprika
- 1/2 tbsp onion powder
- 1/2 tbsp garlic powder
- 1/4 tsp dried cumin
- 2 tbsp apple juice vinegar
- 1/2-1 tsp ocean salt, dark salt or pink Himalayan salt
- 4 cups custom made stalk, bone stock or water
- Olive oil
- S+P to taste

Directions:

1. Attachment in the Instant Pot and press the "Sauté" work.

2. Include the olive oil, onions, carrots, shepherd peppers, and garlic to the pot and sauté until they start to mellow and turn translucent. Add a spot of salt to bring out flavors and discharge juices.

3. When the veggies are delicate mix in the flavors to cover.

4. Include the ACV and join well. Give the vinegar a chance to cook off for a moment or two, blending

persistently. Scrape up any darker bits joined to the base of the pot.

5. Include the container of tomatoes and the cleaved up simmered red peppers to the pot, mix well, and let the tomato blend cook for a moment.

6. Add the greens to the pot just as the cauliflower florets, mix to consolidate, trailed by 4 cups of water (or stalk bone juices).

7. Press the "Keep Warm/Cancel" catch to stop the sauté mode.

8. Mix and afterward place the top on the Instant Pot and lock the top. Curve the steam discharge handle on the top to "Fixing".

9. Press the "Soup" catch to switch the cooking mode. The cooking time will set for 30 minutes. Note that the soup will cook for longer than 30 minutes as it requires some investment for the compel cooker to arrive at the wanted weight. The brief clock will begin once an appropriate weight is accomplished.

More directions to follow:

1. When the soup is finished cooking the Instant Pot will naturally change to the "Keep Warm" mode and will flag finished with signals. When you hear the blares, the soup has cooked for the full 30 minutes

at full weight. Give the soup a chance to stay in the "Keep Warm" mode for 10 minutes and afterward press "Drop."

2. Curve the steam discharge handle on the top to "Venting". I generally put on my broiler glove as a safeguard as a limited quantity of steam will escape from the venting gap.

3. When the weight has discharged, cautiously open the Instant Pot.

4. Test for flavoring. Include progressively pink salt, fresh split pepper, and new pressed lemon juice to taste.

5. Utilize a potato masher to separate the lumps of cauliflower to arrive at desired consistency or mix for a smooth consistency.

6. Scoop soup into bowls. Top with some newly slashed chives and hot red pepper chips if so wants!

CULIFLOWER WEDGES

Total Time

Prep: 22 min. Bake: 40 min.

Makes

4 servings

Ingredients:

- 1 huge head cauliflower
- 1 teaspoon ground turmeric

- 1/2 teaspoon squashed red pepper chips
- 2 tablespoons olive oil
- Lemon juice, extra olive oil, & pomegranate seeds, discretionary

Directions:

1. Remove leaves and trim originate from cauliflower. Cut cauliflower into eight wedges. Blend turmeric and pepper pieces. Brush wedges with oil; sprinkle with turmeric blend.

2. Grill, secured, over medium-high warmth or cook 4 in. from heat until cauliflower is delicate, 9 minutes on each side. Whenever wanted, shower with lemon juice

and extra oil and present with pomegranate seeds.

ROASTED PUMPKIN & BRUSSELS SPROUTS

Total Time

Prep: 15 min. Bake: 35 min.

Makes

8 servings

Ingredients:

- 1 medium pie pumpkin (around 3 pounds), stripped and cut into 3/4-inch 3D shapes
- 1 pound new Brussels grows, cut and split the long way
- 4 garlic cloves, meagerly cut
- 1/3 cup olive oil
- 2 tablespoons balsamic vinegar

- 1 teaspoon ocean salt
- 1/2 teaspoon coarsely ground pepper
- 2 tablespoons minced crisp parsley

Directions:

1. Preheat broiler to 400°. In an enormous bowl, consolidate pumpkin, Brussels sprouts, and garlic. In a little bowl, whisk oil, vinegar, salt, and pepper; shower over vegetables and hurl to cover.

2. Move to a lubed 15x10x1-in. Preparing container. Cook 35-40 minutes or until delicate, blending once. Sprinkle with parsley.

BLACK BEAN-TOMATO CHILI

Total Time

Prep: 10 min. Cook: 35 min.

Makes

6 servings (2-1/4 quarts)

Ingredients:

- 2 tablespoons olive oil
- 1 huge onion, cleaved

- 1 medium green pepper, cleaved
- 3 garlic cloves, minced
- 1 teaspoon ground cinnamon
- 1 teaspoon ground cumin
- 1 teaspoon bean stew powder
- 1/4 teaspoon pepper
- 3 jars (14-1/2 ounces each) diced tomatoes, undrained
- 2 jars (15 ounces each) dark beans, washed and depleted
- 1 cup squeezed orange or juice from 3 medium oranges

Directions:

1. In a Dutch broiler, heat oil over medium-high warmth. Include onion and green pepper; cook and mix 8-10 minutes or until delicate.

Include garlic and seasonings; cook brief longer.

2. Mix in extra fixings; heat to the point of boiling. Lessen heat; stew, secured, 20-25 minutes to enable flavors to mix, blending incidentally.

ROASTED BALSAMIC RED POTATOES

Total Time

Prep: 10 min. Bake: 30 min.

Makes

6 servings

Ingredients:

- 2 pounds little red potatoes, cut into wedges
- 2 tablespoons olive oil
- 3/4 teaspoon garlic pepper mix
- 1/2 teaspoon Italian flavoring
- 1/4 teaspoon salt
- 1/4 cup balsamic vinegar

Directions:

1. Preheat stove to 425°. Hurl potatoes with oil and seasonings; spread in a 15x10x1-in. skillet.
2. Broil 25 minutes, blending midway. Sprinkle with vinegar; cook until potatoes are delicate, 5-10 minutes.

EASY HOMEMADE CHUNKY APPLESAUCE

Total Time

Prep/Total Time: 30 min.

Makes

5 cups

Ingredients:

- 7 medium McIntosh, Empire or different apples (around 3 pounds)
- 1/2 cup sugar
- 1/2 cup water
- 1 tablespoon lemon juice
- 1/4 teaspoon almond or vanilla concentrate
- Fueled by Chicory

Directions

1. Strip, center and cut every apple into 8 wedges. Cut each wedge across down the middle, place in a huge pan. Include remaining fixings.

CHOCOLATE RASPBERRY LAYER CAKE

Cook Time: 60 minutes

Servings: 12

Ingredients:

- 1/2 cup chocolate protein powder
- 1 1/2 cups wholemeal flour
- 2 teaspoons baking powder
- 1 cup cacao powder
- 1 teaspoon baking soda
- 1/2 cup cashews + 1 1/2 cup water
- 1/2 cup coconut nectar
- 1/2 cup coconut oil, melted
- 2 teaspoon vanilla extract
- 2 tablespoon apple cider vinegar
- 3/4 teaspoon sea salt
- 1 cup dates
- 1 cup cashews
- 2/3 cup water
- 2 cups raspberries

Instructions:

1. Preheat the oven to 350 F and grease a cake tin.

2. Grind almonds into flour and mix with chocolate protein powder, 1/2 cup cacao powder, 2 teaspoon baking powder, 1 teaspoon baking soda, 1/2 teaspoon salt and 1/2 cup cashews.

3. Blend coconut nectar, oil, apple cider vinegar and vanilla extract in a blender. Combine the dry and wet ingredients together. Bake for 45 minutes. Remove, let cool 10 minutes then cool completely on a wire rack.

4. Blend the remaining ingredients except for raspberries in a blender until smooth to make ganache.

5. Slice the cake in half, spread half of the ganache on the bottom, place 1 cup raspberries on top, add another half of cake, another half of ganache and the remaining raspberries on top.

6. Let rest for 30 minutes and serve.

PEANUT BUTTER CHIA BARS

Cook Time: 5 minutes

Servings: 2

Ingredients:

- 2 tablespoon chia seeds
- 2 1/2 tablespoon PB2
- 1 tablespoon water
- 3 drops vanilla extract
- 1 tablespoon almonds, chopped

- 1/2 teaspoon honey

Instructions:

1. Mix chia, water, vanilla, honey and PB2 in a bowl.
2. Transfer to a container and flatten. Chop almonds and add to the bars.
3. Serve and enjoy!

HIDDEN GREENS CHOCOLATE PROTEIN SHAKE

Cook Time: 5 minutes

Servings: 3 cups

Ingredients:

- 1 cup frozen kale

- 1 1/2 cups almond milk, unsweetened
- 2 tablespoons hulled hemp seeds
- 3 Medjool dates pitted
- 2 tablespoons cocoa powder
- 1 banana
- 1 tablespoon avocado
- A dash cinnamon

Instructions:

1. Blend all ingredients until smooth.
2. Serve in chilled cups.

CHOCOLATE BLACK BEAN SMOOTHIE

Cook Time: 2 minutes

Servings: 1

Ingredients:

- 1 cup cauliflower, frozen
- 1 banana, frozen
- 1/2 cup black beans
- 1 cup almond milk
- 1/2 Medjool dates
- 1 tablespoon cocoa powder
- 1 tablespoon hemp seeds
- 1 teaspoon ground cinnamon

Instructions:

1. Add all ingredients to a blender and blend until smooth.
2. Transfer to a glass cup and serve.

VEGAN VANILLA CASHEW SHAKE

Cook Time: 5 minutes

Servings: 1

Ingredients:

- 1/3 cup raw cashews

- 1 banana
- 1 tablespoon maple syrup
- 1/3 cup water
- 1/2 teaspoon vanilla extract
- 1 cup of ice cubes
- 1 tablespoon chia seeds
- A pinch salt

Instructions:

1. Add all ingredients to a blender. Blend on low until mixed well. Blend on high for 30 seconds until pureed.
2. Transfer to a glass cup and serve.

EASY PEANUT BUTTER PROTEIN BARS

Cook Time: 5 minutes

Servings: 4-8

Ingredients:

- 3/4 cup honey
- 1 cup peanut butter
- 1 1/2 cups quick oats
- 1 cup vanilla protein powder

Instructions:

1. Line a pan with parchment paper. Heat honey and peanut butter in the microwave for 30 seconds on high and mix to combine. Heat for another 30 seconds and mix.

2. Add protein powder and oats until mixed well. Spread on the prepared pan.

3. Refrigerate for 1 hour. Remove and cut into 12 bars.

4. Serve and enjoy.

VEGAN CHOCOLATE ALMOND PROTEIN BARS

Cook time: 10 minutes

Servings: 4

Ingredients:

- 1 teaspoon cinnamon
- 1 cup raw almonds
- 1 1/2 cups rolled oats
- 1/3 cup maple syrup
- 5 oz. vanilla protein powder
- 1/4 cup chocolate chips, dairy-free
- 1/4 teaspoon salt

Instructions:

1. Line a square pan with parchment paper. Chop 1/4 cup almonds and set aside.

2. Add remaining almonds and salt to a blender and blend for few minutes. Add cinnamon, protein powder, oats, and maple syrup and blend until smooth.

3. Transfer mixture to the pan and spread. Top with the chopped almonds.

4. Add chocolate chips in a bowl and microwave until melted. Add chocolate over the bars and refrigerate for 20 minutes.

5. Cut into bars and serve.

SWEET POTATO-CHICKPEA PATTIES WITH SRIRACHA-YOGURT DIP

Cook time: 15 minutes

Servings: 4

Ingredients:

- 1 sweet potato
- 3 tablespoon vegetable oil
- 15 oz. can garbanzo beans, drained and rinsed
- 1/4 cup panko breadcrumbs
- 1/2 yellow onion
- 2 garlic cloves, minced
- 1 egg, beaten

- 2 tablespoons parsley leaves, chopped
- 1 1/8 teaspoon ground cumin
- 1/2 teaspoon smoked paprika
- 2 teaspoons fine salt
- 1/2 cup Greek yogurt
- 1 1/2 teaspoons Sriracha sauce
- 1/4 teaspoon kosher salt

Instructions:

1. Add garbanzo beans to a bowl and mash until all beans are mashed. Peel and grate the sweet potato and add to the bowl. Grate the onion slightly larger and add to the bowl.

2. Add parsley, garlic, egg, panko, paprika, 1 teaspoon cumin and fine salt in the bowl and mix well.

3. Take 1/4 cup mixture and form into 1/2" thick patties. Heat half oil in a pan over medium heat. Place half of the patties and cook for 4 minutes per side. Remove to a plate and repeat with remaining oil and patties.

4. Mix Sriracha sauce, yogurt, kosher salt and remaining cumin in a bowl.

5. Serve patties with the sauce.

DARK CHOCOLATE HEMP ENERGY BITES

Cook Time: 25 minutes

Servings: 20 bites

Ingredients:

- 2 cups raw walnuts
- 1 cup Medjool dates, pitted
- 3 tablespoon hemp seeds
- 6 tablespoon cacao powder
- 3 tablespoon almond butter
- 1 tablespoon coconut oil, melted
- 1/4 teaspoon sea salt

Instructions:

1. Add dates to a blender and blend until small bits remain. Take out

and set aside. Add walnuts to a blender and blend until smooth. Add hemp seeds, cacao powder, and sea salt. Blend to combine.

2. Add dates back to blender with coconut oil and almond butter. Blend until combined.

3. Refrigerate for 10 minutes. Take out tablespoon amounts and form into 20 balls.

4. Serve and enjoy.

NO-BAKE VEGAN PROTEIN BARS

Cook Time: 40 minutes

Servings: 9 bars

Ingredients:

- 1 cup almond butter
- 2 tablespoon maple syrup
- 1/3 cup amaranth
- 3 tablespoon vanilla vegan protein powder

Instructions:

1. Line a baking pan with parchment paper and set aside.
2. Heat a pot over medium-high heat. Pop amaranth by adding 3 tablespoons at a time and cook for

10 seconds and remove repeat and transfer to a bowl and set aside.

3. Add maple syrup and almond butter to a bowl and mix well. Add protein powder and stir. Add popped amaranth a little at a time until a dough forms. Stir.

4. Transfer the mixture to the baking pan and spread evenly. Lay parchment paper on top and press down to make an even layer.

5. Place in the freezer for 15 minutes.

6. Cut into bars and serve.

RUNNER RECOVERY BITES

Cook time: 10 minutes

Servings: 12

Ingredients:

- 1/4 cup pumpkin seeds, soaked for 1 hour
- 1/3 cup oats
- 1/4 cup sunflower seeds, soaked for 1 hour
- 5 dates
- 1 teaspoon maca powder
- 1 tablespoon goji berries
- 1 teaspoon coconut, shredded and unsweetened
- 1 tablespoon coconut water

- 1 teaspoon vanilla extract
- 1 tablespoon protein powder
- 1 tablespoon maple syrup
- 1/4 cup hemp seeds
- A pinch sea salt

Instructions:

1. Drain sunflower and pumpkin seeds and add to a blender. Blend until a paste forms. Add dates and blend to mix. Add the remaining ingredients except hemp seeds and blend until a dough forms.

2. Roll 1 tablespoon dough into balls with hands. Roll the ball in hemp seeds until covered.

3. Transfer the prepared balls to a plate and freeze until firm.

4. Serve and enjoy.

HIGH PROTEIN VEGAN CHEESY SAUCE

Cook Time: 10 minutes

Servings: 2 cups

Ingredients:

- 1 1/4 cups unsweetened plant-based milk
- 1 block tofu
- 1 teaspoon onion powder
- 2 teaspoon garlic powder
- 1/2 cup nutritional yeast
- 1/4 teaspoon turmeric
- 3/4 teaspoon salt

Instructions:

1. Add all ingredients to a blender and blend until smooth. Combine well. Add more milk as desired.
2. Refrigerate for 24 hours.
3. Serve and enjoy.

VEGAN HIGH-PROTEIN QUESO

Cook time: 5 minutes

Servings: 2

Ingredients:

- 1/4 cup nutritional yeast
- 1/2 block tofu
- 3 tablespoon lemon juice
- 1/4 teaspoon tapioca starch
- 1/4 teaspoon garlic powder
- 1/4 teaspoon turmeric
- 1/4 teaspoon onion powder
- 1/4 cup water
- 1/2 teaspoon salt

Instructions:

1. Add tofu, yeast, starch, lemon juice, salt, garlic powder, turmeric and onion powder and blend until well mixed.

2. Add water as desired. Heat in a microwave for 30 seconds.

3. Serve and enjoy.

VEGAN BUFFALO SAUCE

Cook time: 5 minutes

Servings: 1 cup

Ingredients:

- 1/2 cup soy milk
- 1 cup hot sauce
- 1/2 cup vinegar
- 1/2 teaspoon pepper
- 2 tablespoons sugar
- 1/2 teaspoon garlic granules
- 1 tablespoon tomato sauce

Instructions:

1. Mix soy milk, hot sauce, sugar, vinegar, sugar, pepper, tomato sauce and garlic granules in a pan

and cook over medium heat for 10 minutes.

2. Let cool and serve.

VEGAN RANCH DRESSING (DIPPING SAUCE)

Cook time: 5 minutes

Servings: 8

Ingredients:

- 2 tablespoons lemon juice
- 14 oz. silken tofu
- 1 tablespoon yellow mustard
- 1 tablespoon apple cider vinegar
- 1 teaspoon onion granules
- 1 tablespoon agave
- 1 teaspoon garlic granules
- 2 tablespoons parsley, minced
- 2 tablespoons dill, minced
- 1/2 teaspoon Himalayan salt

Instructions:

1. Add all ingredients except parsley and dill to a blender and blend until smooth at high speed.
2. Add dill and parsley and blend until mixed.
3. Serve chilled.

VEGAN SMOKEY MAPLE BBQ SAUCE

Cook time: 5 minutes

Servings: 8

Ingredients:

- 1 tablespoon maple syrup
- 1/2 cup ketchup
- 1 teaspoon garlic powder
- 1 teaspoon liquid smoke

Instructions:

1. Add all ingredients to a bowl. Mix them until well combined.
2. Serve and enjoy.

VEGAN WHITE BEAN GRAVY

Cook time: 5 minutes

Servings: 2 1/5 cups

Ingredients:

- 1 cup of soy milk
- 1 cup vegetable broth
- 1 cup white beans, rinsed and drained
- 1 tablespoon nutritional yeast
- 3 tablespoons tamari
- 1 teaspoon garlic granules, dried
- 2 teaspoons onion granules, dried
- 2 tablespoons all-purpose flour
- 1 tablespoon combination thyme, oregano, dill, minced

- 1/4 teaspoon black pepper
- 1/4 teaspoon Himalayan salt

Instructions:

1. Add all ingredients except flour, herbs, and salt to a blender and blend on high speed until smooth.
2. Add this mixture to a pan placed over medium heat. Add salt, herbs, and flour, whisk all the time — Cook for 5 minutes.
3. Serve and enjoy.

TAHINI MAPLE DRESSING

Cook time: 5 minutes

Servings: 4 oz

Ingredients

- ¼ cup tahini
- 1 ½ tablespoons maple syrup
- 2 teaspoons lemon juice
- ¼ cup of water
- 1/8 teaspoon Himalayan pink salt

Instructions

1. Add all the ingredients to a bowl, Stir well to combine, until well mixed.
2. Use as a dressing for the salad or other dishes. Store in a fridge.

COCONUT SUGAR PEANUT SAUCE

Cook time: 5 minute

Servings: 1 ½ cups

Ingredients

- 4 tablespoons coconut sugar
- 6 tablespoons powdered peanut butter
- 1 tablespoon chili sauce
- 2 tablespoons liquid aminos
- ¼ cup of water
- 1 teaspoon lime juice
- ½ teaspoon ginger powder

Instructions

1. In a bowl, combine all the ingredients until properly combined. Serve as a topping for the salad or other dishes.
2. Store in a fridge.

COCONUT SAUCE

Cook time: 15 minutes

Servings: 3

Ingredients

- ½ cup red lentils, cooked
- 4 carrots, peeled, chopped

- 1 cup (250 ml) coconut milk, canned
- 3 tablespoons nutritional yeast
- ½ onion, diced
- 2 garlic cloves, minced
- Pepper and salt, to taste

Instructions

1. Boil the carrots for 10 minutes in a pan.
2. Blend the cooked carrots, lentils, onion, garlic, yeast and coconut milk in a blender until smooth. Stir in pepper and salt.
3. Pour the mixture into a saucepan and cook for 2 minutes, stirring frequently.

4. Pour the sauce over the cooked pasta or salad servers.

VEGAN BEAN PESTO

Cook time: 5 minutes

Servings: 2

Ingredients

- 1 can (15 oz.) white beans, drained, rinsed
- 2 cups basil leaves, washed, dried
- ½ cup non-dairy milk
- 2 tablespoons olive oil
- 3 tablespoons nutritional yeast
- 1 garlic clove, peeled
- Pepper and salt to taste

Instructions

1. Blend all the ingredients (except the seasonings) in a blender until smooth.

2. Sprinkle with pepper and salt to taste, then blend for 1 extra minute. Enjoy with pasta.

4 WEEKS MEAL PLAN

Week 1

Day 1

Breakfast Almond Milk Quinoa

Lunch Bean Lentil Salad with Lime Dressing

Dinner Tomato-Braised Lentils with Broccoli Rabe

Dessert Easy Banana-Cacao Ice Cream

Day 2

Breakfast Quinoa and Sweet Potatoes

Lunch Lentil Arugula Salad

Dinner Caesar White Bean Burgers

Dessert Flourless Walnut Kidney Bean Brownies

Day 3

Breakfast Honey Buckwheat Coconut Porridge

Lunch Red Cabbage and Cucumber Salad with Seitan

Dinner Southwestern Quinoa Stuffed Peppers

Dessert Raw Protein Thin Mints

Day 4

Breakfast Tempeh and Potato

Lunch Protein Packed Chickpeas and Kidney Beans Salad

Dinner Tofu Chickpea Stir-Fry with Tahini Sauce

Snack Peanut Butter Chia Bars

Day 5

Breakfast Breakfast French Toast

Lunch Quick Chickpeas and Spinach Salad

Dinner Smoky Tempeh Burrito Bowls

Snack Hidden Greens Chocolate Protein Shake

Day 6

Breakfast Dairy-Free Pumpkin Pancakes

Lunch Carrot Slaw and Tempeh Triangles

Dinner Sweet and Sour Tempeh

Dessert Fudgy Cinnamon Chai Protein Bars

Day 7

Breakfast Protein Blueberry Bars

Lunch Chili Tofu

Dinner Korean Braised Tofu

Snack Chocolate Black Bean Smoothie

Week 2

Day 1

Breakfast Chickpea Scramble Breakfast Basin

Lunch Lentil Soup (Vegan)

Dinner Red Lentil Tikka Masala

Dessert Black Bean Chocolate Orange Mousse

Day 2

Breakfast Quinoa, Oats, Hazelnut and Blueberry Salad

Lunch Hot Black Beans and Potato

Dinner Red Lentil Tikka Masala

Dessert Chocolate Crispy Fruit Squares

Day 3

Breakfast Buttered Overnight Oats

Lunch Low-Fat Bean Soup

Dinner Easy Thai Red Tofu Curry

Dessert Flourless Salted Caramel Chocolate Chip Cookies

Day 4

Breakfast Protein Breakfast Burrito

Lunch Protein Rich Vegetable Minestrone

Dinner Teriyaki Glazed Tofu Steaks

Snack Vegan Vanilla Cashew Shake

Day 5

Breakfast Breakfast Hummus Toast

Lunch Quinoa Pumpkin Soup

Dinner Easy Vegan Chilli Sin Carne

Snack Vegan Vanilla Cashew Shake

Day 6

Breakfast Almond Milk Banana Smoothie

Lunch Red Lentil Soup with Farro

Dinner Teriyaki Tofu Stir Fry Over Quinoa

Dessert Mango Chia Seed Pudding

Day 7

Breakfast Nutritious Toasted Chickpeas

Lunch Moroccan Pumpkin Soup u

Dinner Vegan Fall Farro Protein Bowl

Snack Easy Peanut Butter Protein Bars

Week 3

Day 1

Breakfast Almond Milk Chai Quinoa

Lunch Mexican Chickpea and Tomatillos Pozole

Dinner Black Bean and Quinoa Balls and Spiralized Zucchini

Dessert Banana Bread Cookies

Day 2

Breakfast Tomato Tofu Breakfast Tacos

Lunch Modernized French Onion Soup

Dinner Mongolian Seitan (Vegan Mongolian Beef)

Dessert Simple Baked Cheesecake

Day 3

Breakfast Peanut Butter Oats

Lunch Tofu Bacon Bean Salad

Dinner Teriyaki Tempeh

Dessert Gluten-Free Pear and Banana Loaf

Day 4

Breakfast Protein Pancakes

Lunch Rice Noodles Salad for the Summer

Dinner Vegan Spinach Ricotta Lasagne

Snack Dark Chocolate Hemp Energy Bites

Day 5

Breakfast Savory Vegan Omelet

Lunch Protein Power Salad

Dinner Vegan Samosa Pie

Snack Vegan Chocolate Almond Protein Bars

Day 6

Breakfast Protein Patties

Lunch 'Roomy' Lemon Salad

Dinner Lentil Roast with Balsamic Onion Gravy

Dessert Plant-Based Blueberry Crisp

Day 7

Breakfast Vegan Chickpea Pancake

Lunch All-in-One Roasted Squash and Freekeh Lunch Salad

Dinner Grilled Breaded Tofu Steaks with Spinach Salad

Snack Sweet Potato-Chickpea Patties with Sriracha-Yogurt Dip

Week 4

Day 1

Breakfast Protein Pudding

Lunch Vegan Cauliflower Soup

Dinner Sweet Potato and Black Bean Enchiladas

Dessert Raw Chickpea Cookie Dough

Day 2

Breakfast Gluten-Free Tofu Quiche

Lunch Panzanella

Dinner Edamame Fried Rice

Dessert Whole Food Plant-Based Apple Crisp

Day 3

Breakfast Pumpkin Oatmeal

Lunch Nutritious Beet Hummus

Dinner Vegan Shepherd's Pie with Crispy Cauliflower Crust

Dessert Vegan Chocolate Beet Cake

Day 4

Breakfast Breakfast Berry Quinoa

Lunch White Bean Soup with Green Herb Dumplings

Dinner Hearty Vegetarian Chili with Butternut Squash

Snack Peanut Butter Chia Bars

Day 5

Breakfast Almond Milk Quinoa

Lunch Bean Lentil Salad with Lime Dressing

Dinner Tomato-Braised Lentils with Broccoli Rabe

Snack Runner Recovery Bites

Day 6

Breakfast Quinoa and Sweet Potatoes

Lunch Lentil Arugula Salad

Dinner Caesar White Bean Burgers

Dessert Vegan Blueberry Flax Muffins

Day 7

Breakfast Honey Buckwheat Coconut Porridge

Lunch Red Cabbage and Cucumber Salad with Seitan

Dinner Southwestern Quinoa Stuffed Peppers

Snack No-Bake Vegan Protein Bars

CULIFLOWER WEDGES

Total Time

Prep: 22 min. Bake: 40 min.

Makes

4 servings

Ingredients:

- 1 huge head cauliflower
- 1 teaspoon ground turmeric

- 1/2 teaspoon squashed red pepper chips
- 2 tablespoons olive oil
- Lemon juice, extra olive oil, & pomegranate seeds, discretionary

Directions:

1. Remove leaves and trim originate from cauliflower. Cut cauliflower into eight wedges. Blend turmeric and pepper pieces. Brush wedges with oil; sprinkle with turmeric blend.

2. Grill, secured, over medium-high warmth or cook 4 in. from heat until cauliflower is delicate, 9 minutes on each side. Whenever

wanted, shower with lemon juice and extra oil and present with pomegranate seeds.

ROASTED PUMPKIN & BRUSSELS SPROUTS

Total Time

Prep: 15 min. Bake: 35 min.

Makes

8 servings

Ingredients:

- 1 medium pie pumpkin (around 3 pounds), stripped and cut into 3/4-inch 3D shapes
- 1 pound new Brussels grows, cut and split the long way
- 4 garlic cloves, meagerly cut
- 1/3 cup olive oil
- 2 tablespoons balsamic vinegar
- 1 teaspoon ocean salt

- 1/2 teaspoon coarsely ground pepper
- 2 tablespoons minced crisp parsley

Directions:

1. Preheat broiler to 400°. In an enormous bowl, consolidate pumpkin, Brussels sprouts, and garlic. In a little bowl, whisk oil, vinegar, salt, and pepper; shower over vegetables and hurl to cover.

2. Move to a lubed 15x10x1-in. Preparing container. Cook 35-40 minutes or until delicate, blending once. Sprinkle with parsley.

BLACK BEAN-TOMATO CHILI

Total Time

Prep: 10 min. Cook: 35 min.

Makes

6 servings (2-1/4 quarts)

Ingredients:

- 2 tablespoons olive oil

- 1 huge onion, cleaved
- 1 medium green pepper, cleaved
- 3 garlic cloves, minced
- 1 teaspoon ground cinnamon
- 1 teaspoon ground cumin
- 1 teaspoon bean stew powder
- 1/4 teaspoon pepper
- 3 jars (14-1/2 ounces each) diced tomatoes, undrained
- 2 jars (15 ounces each) dark beans, washed and depleted
- 1 cup squeezed orange or juice from 3 medium oranges

Directions:

1. In a Dutch broiler, heat oil over medium-high warmth. Include

onion and green pepper; cook and mix 8-10 minutes or until delicate. Include garlic and seasonings; cook brief longer.

2. Mix in extra fixings; heat to the point of boiling. Lessen heat; stew, secured, 20-25 minutes to enable flavors to mix, blending incidentally.

ROASTED BALSAMIC RED POTATOES

Total Time

Prep: 10 min. Bake: 30 min.

Makes

6 servings

Ingredients:

- 2 pounds little red potatoes, cut into wedges
- 2 tablespoons olive oil
- 3/4 teaspoon garlic pepper mix
- 1/2 teaspoon Italian flavoring
- 1/4 teaspoon salt
- 1/4 cup balsamic vinegar

Directions:

1. Preheat stove to 425°. Hurl potatoes with oil and seasonings; spread in a 15x10x1-in. skillet.
2. Broil 25 minutes, blending midway. Sprinkle with vinegar; cook until potatoes are delicate, 5-10 minutes.

EASY HOMEMADE CHUNKY APPLESAUCE

Total Time

Prep/Total Time: 30 min.

Makes

5 cups

Ingredients:

- 7 medium McIntosh, Empire or different apples (around 3 pounds)

- 1/2 cup sugar
- 1/2 cup water
- 1 tablespoon lemon juice
- 1/4 teaspoon almond or vanilla concentrate
- Fueled by Chicory

Directions

1. Strip, center and cut every apple into 8 wedges. Cut each wedge across down the middle, place in a huge pan. Include remaining fixings.

2. Heat to the point of boiling. Diminish excitement; stew, secured until wanted consistency is come to,

15-20 minutes, mixing once in a while.

MUSHROOM & BROCCOLI SOUP

Total Time

Prep: 20 min. Cook: 45 min.

Makes

8 servings

Ingredients:

- 1 bundle broccoli (around 1-1/2 pounds)

- 1 tablespoon canola oil
- 1/2 pound cut crisp mushrooms
- 1 tablespoon diminished sodium soy sauce
- 2 medium carrots, finely slashed
- 2 celery ribs, finely slashed
- 1/4 cup finely slashed onion
- 1 garlic clove, minced
- 1 container (32 ounces) vegetable juices
- 2 cups of water
- 2 tablespoons lemon juice

Directions:

1. Cut broccoli florets into reduced down pieces. Strip and hack stalks.

2. In an enormous pot, heat oil over medium-high warmth; saute mushrooms until delicate, 4-6 minutes. Mix in soy sauce; expel from skillet. In the same container, join broccoli stalks, carrots, celery, onion, garlic, soup, and water; heat to the point of boiling. Diminish heat; stew, revealed, until vegetables are relaxed, 25-30 minutes. Puree soup utilizing a drenching blender. Or then again, cool marginally and puree the soup in a blender; come back to the dish. Mix in florets and mushrooms; heat to the point of boiling. Lessen warmth to medium; cook until

broccoli is delicate, 8-10 minutes, blending infrequently. Mix in lemon juice.

AVOCADO FRUIT SALAD WITH TANGERINE VINAIGRETTE

Total Time

Prep/Total Time: 25 min.

Makes

8 servings

Ingredients:

- 3 medium ready avocados, stripped and meagerly cut
- 3 medium mangoes, stripped and meagerly cut
- 1 cup crisp raspberries
- 1 cup crisp blackberries
- 1/4 cup minced crisp mint
- 1/4 cup cut almonds, toasted

DRESSING:

- 1/2 cup olive oil
- 1 teaspoon ground tangerine or orange strip
- 1/4 cup tangerine or squeezed orange
- 2 tablespoons balsamic vinegar
- 1/2 teaspoon salt

- 1/4 teaspoon naturally ground pepper

Directions:

1. Mastermind avocados and organic product on a serving plate; sprinkle with mint and almonds. In a little bowl, whisk dressing fixings until mixed; shower over a plate of mixed greens.

2. To toast nuts, prepare in a shallow container in a 350° stove for 5-10 minutes or cook in a skillet over low warmth until softly sautéed, mixing every so often.

CPSIA information can be obtained
at www.ICGtesting.com
Printed in the USA
BVHW090036120521
607047BV00002B/224

9 781802 232462